THE GREAT HIGHWAY

First published in 1990 by Absolute Classics, an imprint of
Absolute Press, 14 Widcombe Crescent, Bath, England

© Eivor Martinus

Series Editor: Giles Croft

Cover and text design: Ian Middleton

Photoset and printed by WBC Print, Bristol
Bound by W.H. Ware & Son, Clevedon

ISBN 0 948230 00 0

THE GREAT HIGHWAY

August Strindberg

Translated by Eivor Martinus

absolute classics

INTRODUCTION

Strindberg's last play, THE GREAT HIGHWAY, (Stora Landsvägen) written in 1909 when he was sixty years old, is an odd mixture of bizarre comedy and serious drama divided into seven loosely connected episodes. The satirical passages (Scenes Two, Three and Four) have a surreal quality bordering on the absurd which shows an uncanny resemblance to Samuel Beckett.

The extraordinary thing about this play is that it turns out to be a sample of all the various techniques employed by Strindberg during his forty years as a playwright. In the tender sixth scene, *At the Last Gate*, where The Hunter, the main character, recalls the happiness he experienced with his young daughter, the tone is soft and melancholy: "happiness does exist, but it is brief like lightning, like sunshine, like the convolvulus which flowers for one day and then no more!"

In the first and last scenes, on the other hand, the grandeur of nature and religion is mirrored in Strindberg's lyrical monologues. As so often with Strindberg the form is made to fit the motif, even if that means changing gear at break-neck speed from scene to scene.

THE GREAT HIGHWAY has been compared with two earlier 'Pilgrimage' plays, TO DAMASCUS and A DREAM PLAY, but in this last, his sixty-fifth play, he is more radical, more experimental than previously. Some critics have seen THE GREAT HIGHWAY as a metaphor for Strindberg's life. The author opens the door to his past and the most poignant moments of his life take on a heightened exaggerated importance, displayed either as totally without meaning or with a sinister symbolism acknowledged but not quite understood by The Hunter. In the fourth scene where a Japanese man asks the Hunter to give him the *coup de grâce* there is a visionary moment when the Japanese reveals that his name is Hiroshima. "I have lived, erred and suffered under the name of Hiroshima, the town of my birth," he says and now he wants to feel "the cleansing power of the fire for a short moment . . . suffer . . . and then the liberating bliss."

When the absurdity of human existence is enacted in Scenes Two, Three and Four, Strindberg adopts a terse, clipped nonsensical dialogue, but when he eulogizes over the beauty of nature in Scene One and describes the struggle with the Eternal One in the last scene, the monologues attempt to match their elevated subject. And in the moving scene, *At the last gate* the innocence of the child is depicted in stark, simple language.

THE GREAT HIGHWAY has proved an almost insuperable obstacle to directors over the years. Ingmar Bergman's protégé Peter Stormare presented a highly praised production of the play at The Royal Dramatic Theatre, Stockholm in the autumn of 1989, and the play was also staged in Copenhagen recently in a completely Beckettian vein. In England the play was performed briefly at the experimental theatre, The Watergate, in 1950 but apart from that it has never been professionally staged in Great Britain.

When the play was first published in 1909 it quickly ran into three editions. This was most unusual for a Strindberg play at that time and ever since it has been a popular play with the reading public. It has often been interpreted as yet another dream play, but I think its disjointed form and absurd characters, coupled with a reflective mood and occasional lyrical passages could equally well be interpreted as a last review of life seen through the eyes of a dying man. In the final scene, called *A dark forest*, The Woman asks The Hunter: "And now you are dead?" He answers: "In a civil sense, yes, but spiritually no. I struggle, therefore I live."

The play is made up of a kaleidoscope of images, some distorted, some blurred and some made more beautiful by memory. The Hunter, Strindberg's alter ego, looks back on his life for the last time and singles out the pain, the suffering, the illusions, deceptions, loves, friendships and struggles which finally made him into the man he is, "not the man he'd hoped to be".

We have learnt to associate Strindberg with the Naturalistic and to some extent the Expressionist Movement, but he broke with tradition as early as 1872 when he decided to write his first historical play in prose rather than verse as was then the custom. He presented the Swedish religious reformer Master Olof as a modern rebel who could have sprung straight from the Paris commune of 1871. His Protestant fervour was a disguise for the growing Socialist movement in Europe. Not surprisingly, the play MASTER OLOF had to wait ten years before any Swedish theatre wanted to put it on. In the meantime, Strindberg went bankrupt in 1879 but soon after he had his break-through as a writer with the hugely successful satirical novel, THE RED ROOM.

By that time he had married Siri von Essen and she was working as an actress at the Royal Dramatic Theatre. After a few years they moved abroad with their three children and spent the rest of the eighties in France, Switzerland, Germany and Denmark.

During one happy spell at an artists' colony outside Paris Strindberg became friends with Zola and Gauguin and it was after this period (and when the marriage to Siri was beginning to show signs of strain) that he created the first naturalistic dramas: THE FATHER, MISS JULIE (which ought to be called Lady Julie) and CREDITORS. None of them was an immediate success but that did not deter Strindberg. He carried on with a series of nine one-act plays, including THE STRONGER and the lesser known MOTHERLY LOVE, PARIAH and THE FIRST WARNING which were produced at the Gate Theatre, London in 1985.

This tremendously productive period did not yield any money so Strindberg sat down to write his most successful novel, THE PEOPLE OF HEMSÖ which finally earned him critical acclaim, but by then his first marriage was already on the rocks. It was finally dissolved in 1892 and Siri was given custody of the children.

The early nineties saw a return to bachelor life in Berlin where Strindberg spent most of his time in cafés with other writers and artists. Before long a rich girl, twenty years his junior, fell in love with him and promised to launch him with the help of her father's contacts and money. The relationship was intellectually stimulating and resulted in a brief marriage and another daughter, but his financial situation did not improve, and Strindberg soon set off for Paris to try his luck as a painter. He had encountered the new Impressionists in France and was fascinated by their style. Although Strindberg's attempts at painting were scorned by his contemporaries he seems to have been viewed more kindly by posterity because two of his paintings from this period each fetched over 1.3 million pounds in 1989.

With two ex-wives and four children to support, Strindberg decided to take fate into his own hands and in 1894 he started to practise alchemy. He experimented in a laboratory in Paris but his hands suffered so badly that he had to be treated in hospital for a few weeks. The Swedish Church made a collection to pay for the treatment because Strindberg was completely destitute at this time.

The years that followed have been called his Inferno period after an autobiographical novel by that name. Strindberg had reached rock bottom in every respect and he finally abandoned atheism for his own personal brand of Christianity. He even contemplated entering a monastery but in the end he decided that he could not do without the company of women so he returned to Sweden in time for his fiftieth birthday after having spent almost twenty years abroad.

At the turn of the new century his novels and short stories were reprinted and he finally began to make some money. It was during this period that he wrote his first 'pilgrimage' plays, TO DAMASCUS and A DREAM PLAY, and his confessional drama EASTER.

On his return to Sweden he had fallen in love again with a pretty young actress in her early twenties, Harriet Bosse. She went on to become one of Sweden's leading actresses. Harriet was an enchanting creature and Strindberg was obsessed by her long after the marriage had foundered.

The first decade of the new century saw a flurry of activity as Strindberg, the playwright, was given proper recognition at last. Some of his best History plays were written during this time, like GUSTAV III, QUEEN KRISTINA and GUSTAV ADOLF, but also such diverse plays as SWANWHITE, THE CROWN BRIDE, A DREAM PLAY and DANCE OF DEATH. With the advent of the Intimate Theatre in 1907 a lifelong dream was realised and Strindberg was able to supply his own little theatre with a collection of tailor-made dramas. He used the term 'Chamber plays' because he wanted to apply the idea of chamber music to the art of drama. A single motif, repeated and developed and written in one long act often in the shape of a sonata with a coda at the end became Strindberg's contribution to the new Intimate Theatre.

Strindberg wrote five chamber plays in all: OVÄDER (Thunder in the Air), BRÄNDA TOMTEN (After the Fire), SPÖKSONATEN (The Ghost Sonata), PELIKANEN (The Pelican) and SVARTA HANDSKEN (The Black Glove). Most of them are virtually unknown in this country, partly due to the fact that they have been out of print for years. THE PELICAN was the first play to be produced at The Intimate Theatre, but again Strindberg was too much ahead of his time and his new experiment in drama left the audiences and the critics rather baffled. The theatre only survived for three years even though Strindberg himself invested large sums of money in it. It must have been a disappointed Strindberg who sat down to write his last play, THE GREAT HIGHWAY, in 1909. His beloved theatre which he had waited so long for was not turning out a success after all, he was still spurned by the Establishment and ridiculed by leading critics, his three wives were gone and of his five children he was only seeing the two daughters of his first marriage. On his sixtieth birthday in January 1909 he met his youngest daughter for the first time in two years. When she turned up for his birthday lunch, he cried with happiness.

His greatest pleasures in life at this time were his children and the musical evenings in his home when he played Beethoven with some friends. Those evenings became the highlights of his later years. After a couple of hours' playing, the landlady would turn up with a simple supper and some good wine.

The GREAT HIGHWAY was Strindberg's 'Farewell to life and a personal statement'. He wanted to put on record the passion, love, affection, disillusionment, resentment, beauty in nature, knowledge of God that he had experienced in his lifetime. He also wanted to illuminate the injustices in society, the stupidity of the ruling class and the betrayals that he had witnessed. The result is this 'Pilgrimage drama' in seven episodes, seen as a journey through life with seven stations to the grave. Many of the details were based on real-life events or characters and some of them have lost their significance today. The play would probably benefit if they were cut, but this is how the complete unabridged version looks in all its turmoil. If it comes across as strange, let me assure you that Strindberg is no less strange in Swedish.

In a literal sense, the title THE GREAT HIGHWAY refers to the street where Strindberg used to live as a child and where his coffin was to be carried to the new cemetery north of the city in 1912.

EIVOR MARTINUS

CHARACTERS

HUNTER

HERMIT

WANDERER

MILLER A.

MILLER E.

MILLER'S WIFE

GIRL

SCHOOLMASTER

BLACKSMITH

ORGAN GRINDER

PHOTOGRAPHER

EUPHROSYNE (His wife)

GOTTHARD (Their son)

KLARA (The florist)

JAPANESE MAN

MÖLLER

CHILD

WOMAN

TEMPTER

(Translator's note: The play can be done with six actors, two actresses and a young child.)

SCENE ONE

In the Alps.

A signpost with two "arms", one pointing upwards, the other downwards. At the back, dark thunder clouds. Later on the thunder breaks.

HUNTER: *(Enters, looks at the roadsign.)*
Where am I and how far have I got?

Ah, there's one road going up and another going down.
You always end up down, anyway . . . I want to climb.
But the signpost here opens his arms
as if warning me about the upper road.
Take care! There are many dangers on
the steep and narrow path.
It doesn't worry me. I love the danger.
But first I want to stop awhile
and catch my breath,
collect my thoughts, compose myself
and rediscover me
the ME that was abducted . . .

*

I spent too long among the people
and forgot about my soul,
my heart, my thoughts;
the rest was taken from me . . . stolen
they pinioned me with kindness,
with gifts I didn't want . . .
yes, it was warm walking about down there,
going from home to home, sitting down at beautiful tables,
music and flowers, candles and glass.
But in the end it got too stuffy . . .
so I cut off the moorings
and threw away my ballast
all the things that weighed me down –
what a relief – and look . . . I rose.
Here I can breathe again and give
my tender lungs an airing,
no dust or smoke or other people's breath
to poison my blood.

Pure, white snow
of sublimated steam. Water diamonds,
you lilies, petrified with cold,
you heavenly flour sieved through the black
head-dress of the clouds –
you blessed silence pull your satin quilt
over the tired pilgrim's head
when he goes to bed whispering his prayer.

*

What's to the north? A quarry,
a cloud like the blackboard at school
with nothing written on it. – There's a noise!
The teacher's coming!
And the class is silent.
Silence in nature when the great Teacher speaks!
Look now! A lightning from east to west . . .
He writes his name in letters of fire
on a lead-black cloud! I know you,
the eternal one . . . invisible yet perceivable . . .
severe, all-merciful . . .
And the mountain pines bow
and the streams don't make a sound.
The chamois kneels down in fear
a bare-headed vulture squats with a bald pate
on the ridge of the Alps. . . . Nature trembles.
I . . . called the lord of creation . . .
a nick-name given to me . . .
I succumb in shame, a mere nobody before your
    omnipotence.

*

Look, the cloud burst, the veil is parted.
What's revealed?
The fair earth. The temptress
who draws me back down there.
How pretty you look . . .
dressed in hopeful green, and faithful blue
and lovers' rosy red.
The tall pine trees painted by the sunset
the cypresses of graves and nights
a rock with a temple of marble.
raised as a monument to glory or happiness . . .

A cave, home of the grey sorceress
who frightens the nymphs into the olive grove . . .

Here comes the sun! How it glistens
from frosty rose diamonds; the clouds are trimmed
with silver ribbons, the blue-black cloaks
hung up in the wind to air.
What is that stirring? Who is in the way of the sun?
Who casts a shadow on the white snow?
A golden eagle, chrysaëtos with his golden breast.
The knight of the sky in golden armour
with the chain of chivalry around his neck.
What! Are you coming down? Descending into the valley?
Have your wings got tired . . . perhaps the rudder cannot steer
for the summit?
Yes, he wants to come down, down to rest and mingle
with the crowd, and enjoy the scent of clover-fields . . .
It is still summer down there . . .
Water falls from the clouds like pearls over there . . .
here it's like diamonds, precious stones;
there the stream is warbling but here it's struck dumb . . .
here deserted snow-fields with white flowers . . .
down there white daisies . . .
up here and down there . . . here and there
one's drawn between equal good and equal bad.

*

HERMIT: Where are you going? *Quo vadis*, pilgrim?
            You've covered half the distance and now you look back.
            So far your motto has been Excelsior.

HUNTER: It still is.

HERMIT: What are you looking for up here?

HUNTER: My self . . . which I lost down there.

HERMIT: What you've lost down there surely can't be
            retrieved up here?

HUNTER: You're right. But if I go back down there
            I'll lose even more and I'll never find what I lack.

HERMIT: You want to save your own skin . . .

HUNTER: Not my skin, but my soul . . .

HERMIT: You're not very fond of people . . .

HUNTER: I love them too much. That's why they frighten me as
            well . . .

HERMIT: Loving means giving . . . give!

HUNTER: They don't want to receive my gifts alone . . .
            they want to take the giver too.

HERMIT: The shepherd gave himself for his herd . . .

HUNTER: Yes, dust to dust . . . but the spirit belongs to God.

HERMIT: You're skilled with words. Why don't you put it down
                on paper?
            In any case, your life is only half spent.
            Don't rush the foetus, a premature birth
            will never make you into a man, a human being.
            Go down once more . . . and stay your full term,
            there's nothing to fear.
            The road is dusty . . . you can brush it off,
            the road is lined by ditches . . . step into them.
            But get up again. There are gates and fences . . .
            jump over, crawl under or lift the latch.
            When you meet people, take them in your arms,
            they won't bite, but even if they did it wouldn't hurt.
            If you get splashed with mud, leave it to dry.
            Part with your money, you'll get it back,
            up here there's nothing to be gained,
            because stones are stones and snow is snow –
            but people . . . that is different.

HUNTER: I know, if only I could remain
            a spectator and stay in the audience,
            but I want to get up there on the stage and act, take part
            and as soon as I take on a character
            I forget who I really am . . .

HERMIT: Who are you?

HUNTER: Enough! Let's leave it now . . .
            it's getting too cold for me up here.

HERMIT: And the air a trifle thin . . . and it's lonely . . .
            Look out, we've got company.

HUNTER: A strange fellow. He's coming from up there

and looks a little worse for wear . . .
I say . . . excuse me . . .

*

WANDERER: I've come from the head of the Alps
            where I've . . . immersed myself in air
            but you can't stay immersed forever,
            you've got to put on your clothes and walk on . . .
            – with or without a companion – preferably with, of course.
            Can you tell me what that country in the distance is
                called?

HERMIT: It's called the Land of Wishes.

WANDERER: The Land of Pious Wishes?

HERMIT: Pious and impious according to . . .

WANDERER: Whoever . . .
            I see. I've got a companion.
            Whom do I have the pleasure of . . .

HUNTER: I am a soldier.

WANDERER: And I am a wanderer.
            It is always best to travel incognito . . .
            one should never get too close . . .
            only make acquaintances.
            You never get too close anyway
            it's just a fallacy. . . . So . . .
            companionship without friendship . . . but not with
            hostility either,
            two steps apart, not too close . . . onwards.
            And downwards . . . then straight on!
            Uphill, downhill . . .
            a rest, a tavern, a glass of something
            but steer straight to the south!

HUNTER: With the sun as a lighthouse we won't get lost.
            Its light won't go out and its keeper
            will never fall asleep.
            I believe he's gone, our hermit friend.

WANDERER: Let him go. He doesn't belong down there
            where we are going.
            He has made his choice, and said farewell to the world.

HUNTER: Perhaps he's done the right thing.

WANDERER: Don't look that way.
               The world is full of knaves and it's all one . . .
               here and there and everywhere . . . but we are going there!

SCENE TWO

At the windmills.

An overcast sky at the back. On either side of the stage a windmill, one called Adam, the other Eve. To the right a tavern.
The Wanderer and the Hunter are sitting at a table with a drink each.

WANDERER: It's quiet down here in the valley.

HUNTER: A bit too quiet according to the miller . . .

WANDERER: . . . who is always asleep, regardless of how much water
               runs through his mill . . .

HUNTER: . . . because he is chasing after wind . . .

WANDERER: . . . a futile exercise . . . which has put me off
               windmills altogether . . .

HUNTER: Like the noble knight Don Quixote of La Mancha . . .

WANDERER: . . . who didn't trim his sails to every wind . . .

HUNTER: . . . on the contrary . . .

WANDERER: . . . that's why he got into difficulties. Is this supposed
               to be a kind of "beggar my neighbour"?

HUNTER: Mister Incognito, why do you drink so much?

WANDERER: Because I am always on the operating table. So I need
               an anaesthetic.

HUNTER: I won't ask any more questions.

WANDERER: Maybe I let the cat out of the bag.

HUNTER: I can't make you out.

WANDERER: Don't bother. It's better if you don't.

HUNTER: I suppose so . . . it's been cloudy all day today.

WANDERER: I'll have a few more drinks . . . then it will clear up.

(Drinks) Do you know Greek? Do you know what '*oinos*' means?

HUNTER: '*Oinos*' means wine.

WANDERER: That's right. So you're an educated man?

HUNTER: *Noli me tangere!* Don't touch me. I'm prickly.

WANDERER: Have you noticed how grapes resemble bottles and the tendril looks just like a corkscrew. It's a clear '*signatura*'.

HUNTER: But the juice from the grapes possesses none of the qualities of chloroform. . . .

WANDERER: . . . until the grape has been trodden and left to rot in its dregs, that is,

HUNTER: . . . in order to release the spirit from the soiled skin of matter . . .

WANDERER . . . so it can rise to the surface like seafoam . . .

HUNTER: . . . the stuff Aphrodite sprang from. . . .

WANDERER: . . . disrobed!

HUNTER: Without as much as a vine-leaf to cover herself with . . .

WANDERER: . . . clothes only came with the Fall of Man. Are you always as serious as this?

HUNTER: Are you always such a joker?

WANDERER: Who is the most curious of us two?

HUNTER: Look, how he holds out his arms . . .

WANDERER: . . . subjected to the general laws of attraction . . .

HUNTER: . . . which are followed by mutual repulsion.

WANDERER: A good reason for keeping a distance of two paces, and for marching in open column . . .

HUNTER: . . . according to the agreement dated as above. Stop. Here are the players!

★

WANDERER: May I borrow your eyeglasses. I can't see very well.

★

What does the glass reveal? – It looks like hoar frost,
crystallized water, or salt;
a tear that's dried . . . hot at source
it cooled down fast and turned into rock salt;
the steeled rim has got rusty.
That means he often cries, but secretly,
the tears have dug two furrows from
the eyes to the corners of his mouth
and stopped the smile from bursting
into laughter.
Poor man, your mask is worn
And when you show your teeth
it's difficult to know
whether you intend to bite or smile.

HUNTER: Here begins the play. An idyll with windmills . . .

WANDERER: A pastoral in a minor-major key; here we go!

*

MILLER A.:   Well, today we're on an equal footing as there's no
wind at all, but I'm going to have your mill removed
because it's affecting my trade adversely.

MILLER E.:   You mean I take the easterly wind from you? But you
take the westerly wind from me so we're quits.

MILLER A.:   My windmill was there first and you built yours to
spite me. Now that things are going badly for us both,
wouldn't it be better if one of us prospered at least.

MILLER E.:   You, you mean?

MILLER A.:   You, you mean?

MILLER E.:   Yes, of course.

MILLER A.:   But I meant one of us, the worthiest, the one with
justice on his side.

MILLER E.:   And who would that be?

MILLER A.:   Is that for us to decide, do you think?

MILLER E.:   I know more about grain than you . . . and my Eve
grinds faster, it also carries newer sails . . . and the
wheels turn more quickly.

MILLER A.:   My Adam was built before yours, my mill-bolt is made of boxwood . . .

MILLER E.:   Stop! Let's ask the two gentlemen over there.

WANDERER: Here we go. Now we're bound to get mixed up.

HUNTER: They'll want us to act as witnesses and maybe as judges too so they can pass judgement on our judgement.

MILLER'S
WIFE A.:   Come and have your dinner now, love.

MILLER A.:   Wait a minute.

WIFE A.:   No, the dinner can't wait.

MILLER A.:   You must learn never to be in a hurry.

WIFE A.:   Never?

MILLER A.:   Never . . . the hasty bitch brings forth blind whelps.

WIFE A.:   But the cabbage is getting cold.

MILLER A.:   Are we having cabbage for dinner?
That's a different kettle of fish. I'll be right with you.

WIFE A.:   That means the bitch will bring forth blind whelps.

MILLER A.:   Did I say that? I take it back.

They exit.

WANDERER: He sold his birthright.

HUNTER: . . . for a dish of cabbage.

WANDERER: And it tasted nice.

HUNTER: But here comes the other miller; look how he hovers and preys on us – he wants something from us, some information perhaps. Look, how he scrutinizes us, examines our clothes, shoes, hair and beards. He is a thief.

MILLER E.:   Excuse me . . .

WANDERER: Now he wants to trick us into speaking. Don't answer him.

MILLER E.:   Where do you two gentlemen come from?

WANDERER: It's none of your business.

MILLER E.:   In a strict sense, of course you're right.

WANDERER: We are strict . . . here . . . so why don't you leave us alone.

MILLER E.:   I have no intention of taking anything from you.

WANDERER: That wouldn't be too easy anyway.

MILLER E.:   I was going to give you something . . .

WANDERER: We don't need anything.

MILLER E.:   There's a thing! I was going to give it away free . . . just some information. Important information, mind you! *(Pause)* They are about to blast a rock behind us. *(Pause)* And in a moment the stones will explode all over us.

Hunter and Wanderer get up.

WANDERER: Why didn't you say that at once?

MILLER E.:   You didn't want to hear. But sit down . . . there is no hurry. The men will give us a signal before they start.

WANDERER: Is this the road to the Chosen Land?

MILLER E.:   Yes, this is the most direct route.

WANDERER: What's the forecast for this afternoon?

MILLER E.:   We can expect more thunder; the weather is very unsettled around here.

WANDERER: All the year round?

MILLER E.:   It's always unsettled, all the year round. Year in, year out.

WANDERER: What's the name of the next village?

MILLER E.:   It's none of your business. It is indeed more blessed to give than to take but it's no fun being robbed. Thief! Have you got a passport?

WANDERER: What do we need a passport for?

MILLER E.:   There are robbers in the area and if you can't show us where you've come from you will be strip-searched.

*

HUNTER: What did I say? Now we're thoroughly involved.

WANDERER: It doesn't exactly look like a country idyll.

MILLER E.:   I'll go and fetch my neighbour and his servants and we
               shall soon find an alibi . . .

WANDERER: That's a strange way of going about it.

MILLER E.:   I'm the sheriff here you see, and my neighbour is a
               member of the jury . . .

               Exits.

WANDERER: And now they'll be friends, Herod and Pontius Pilate!

HUNTER: I had hoped to find myself but he who wants to find
               something shall lose it. So here we go . . . back into the
               crowd . . .

WANDERER: . . . where we might sink . . .

HUNTER: . . . but surface again . . .

WANDERER: . . . thanks to a certain life-buoy which sensible people
               carry around them. A woman!

               The girl enters.

HUNTER: . . . as could be expected next to Adam and Eve.

WANDERER: But it doesn't mean that we're in paradise.

HUNTER: Enough. Here we go!

                              *

WANDERER: I think it's better to attack . . . And what's a pretty
               girl like you called?

GIRL: Guess!

WANDERER: Let me see! Blonde, miller's daughter, short of stature,
               round face. You must be called Amalia!

GIRL: How did you know?

WANDERER: I could tell!

GIRL: What if I'd been dark, tall, oval-faced and the daughter
               of a blacksmith? What name would you have given me
               then?

WANDERER: Jenny, of course!

GIRL: That's right!

WANDERER: Now I've taught you something. What will you give me in return?

GIRL: I'll give you . . . a chance of telling me where you've picked up this talent for reading people.

WANDERER: Life, experience, some books, a built-in superior intelligence and a good portion of observational skills. I'm curious to know why you don't want to marry the other miller's son?

GIRL: So you know about that as well!

WANDERER: I think you should take him. That would solve the whole problem with the mills without anyone having to resort to court proceedings – you sell your windmill and move it to the next village where it might be more useful.

GIRL: How clever, how clever you are . . .

WANDERER: But I can tell by your expression that you're not interested in the miller's son. I think you'd prefer one of the highwaymen? Someone with black eyes and black moustaches . . .

GIRL: You frighten me . . . are you a fortune-teller?

WANDERER: As you've gathered, but I can only tell young people's fortunes.

GIRL: Why is that?

WANDERER: Because old people are so cunning.

GIRL: *(To the Hunter.)* Is that true?

WANDERER: Don't bother him; he doesn't want to get involved. Speak to me instead. I would like a little something from you in exchange for all the knowledge I've imparted. You owe me something, you know. You don't want to be in that position, do you?

GIRL: I shall give you something alright – a piece of my mind! I shall make sure you leave this place a wiser man than you arrived. And what's more . . . I want nothing in return . . .

WANDERER: Now there's a thing!

GIRL: Firstly, I'm not called Amalia . . .

WANDERER: . . . but Jenny. What did I say?

GIRL: No, not that either! Secondly, the miller hasn't got a
            son. Thirdly, there are already four windmills in the
            next village so moving our mill wouldn't solve the
            problem. Furthermore, I advise you not to call a
            strange girl by her first name. You never know
            who she might be, even though you think you're so
            clever at guessing. And lastly, don't be disloyal to your
            friend as soon as a third person turns up . . . you may
            live to regret it.

WANDERER: I haven't been disloyal.

GIRL: Yes, you tried to ridicule him just now in order to
            make an impression on me – and that wasn't very nice.
            Now you're on the defensive and if you were to ask my
            name again I wouldn't tell you. Like just now when the
            miller wanted to warn you about the highwaymen.

HUNTER: *(Rises)* Can I offer you a seat, Miss?

GIRL: That's right. You should call me Miss, because my
            father is the lord of the manor and not the miller. *(To
            the Wanderer.)* Go to the miller and mention my name
            and he'll give you a passport. Just say that . . . the
            young lady sent you.

WANDERER: But I must know your name.

GIRL: *(Sits down.)* I don't give away my name to complete
            strangers, and if you're a gentleman, you won't ask for
            it either. Off you go!

            The Wandererer exits.

                              ★

GIRL: You're lucky travelling around and meeting lots of
            people and getting to know so many . . .

HUNTER: Getting to know?

GIRL: That's true. One doesn't really . . . one gets acquainted
            . . .

HUNTER: Hardly that even. But guessing riddles is also a
            pastime.

GIRL: It's pretty useless talk.

HUNTER: You have to translate it! All languages are foreign and
            we're all foreigners to someone. Everyone travels
            incognito.

GIRL: Incognito to ourselves as well. You've suffered a loss
            but you're not dressed in black.

HUNTER: And you're dressed like a miller's daughter but call
            yourself Miss.

GIRL: What about your friend?

HUNTER: He's just an acquaintance. I don't know him at all.

GIRL: What do you think of him?

HUNTER: All and nothing. I haven't worked him out yet.

GIRL: What did you do up there?

HUNTER: Breathed fresh air and tried to forget.

GIRL: But why forget? Without memories life would be
            nothing but a void . . .

HUNTER: . . . but memories are the cargo that makes the ship sink.

GIRL: A ship without cargo is overturned more easily . . .

HUNTER: . . . that's why it is customary to take ballast . . .

GIRL: And reduce the sails.

HUNTER: The same applies to windmills . . .

GIRL: . . . or the wings might break . . .

HUNTER: But the wheels turn fastest when the mill is placed on a
            hill.

GIRL: Best of all in the valleys or the plains.

HUNTER: Where the air is so clear . . .

GIRL: . . . that you can see the charcoal stacks
            and count the parish churches with the naked eye,
            and all the stars of the night appear . . .

HUNTER: . . . not on the horizon . . .

GIRL: . . . but at the zenith. And the zenith will be
               everywhere once you've reached the horizon.

HUNTER: When do I reach the horizon?

GIRL: This very morning you've reached the goal you strived
               for. Isn't it lovely to discover new things once you've
               conquered the old?

HUNTER: But that country in the distance?

GIRL: If you hurry, you'll get there.
               But if you grow weary it will recede . . .
               The Northern star has never had a mortal at the zenith,
               but people go there and return . . . and others make the
               same journey but are forced back. Follow their example
               but learn from your experience.

HUNTER: One drags and dredges one's nose in the nadir . . .

GIRL: But gazes now and again at the zenith.

               The sound of a bugle.

HUNTER: *(Listens)* Listen!

GIRL: I heard, but I don't understand.

HUNTER: I'll translate it for you. You only hear the sounds, but I
               hear the words.

GIRL: What does the brass say?

HUNTER: "Answer my call, where are you, where are you?"

               The bugle answers "Here".

GIRL: Someone is calling you.

               New signal.

HUNTER: "Follow me, this way. Follow me. This way. This
               way."

GIRL: I can hear you're a soldier. Or rather, I can tell by
               looking at you. Someone is calling you. Our parting is
               brief . . . like our meeting.

HUNTER: Not quite so brief. Not quite so easy . . .
               Come with me part of the way to the next village.

GIRL: What about your friend?

HUNTER: You can find people like him in every tavern.

GIRL: You're callous.

HUNTER: I've been in wars. There the motto is Onwards, not Stay.

GIRL: That's why I take my leave.

HUNTER: If you leave, you'll take something with you.

GIRL: And if I stay, you'll take something from me.

HUNTER: *(Looks into the distance.)* Look! They're quarrelling. In a moment they'll be fighting. Here they go! And they'll call me in as a witness. But you must go. You mustn't get mixed up in this.

GIRL: So you care about me?

HUNTER: I care about you . . . I'm full of care . . . for you . . . Good-bye.
            A flower seen through the garden fence
            which gives a moment's pleasure to the passer-by,
            is loveliest when unbroken, when spreading its scent
            with the wind . . . one brief moment and then it's gone.
            Now onwards!

GIRL: Good-bye! Onwards!

            Exit.

                              *

HUNTER: Now I'm grounded. Tied, trapped, pulled into the grindmill of justice, enmeshed in an emotional network, allied with a stranger and drawn into an affair which has nothing to do with me.

WANDERER: Are you still here? I thought you had gone but you must be the faithful type.

HUNTER: Did you get into a fight?

WANDERER: I gave the miller a good talking-to for pulling my leg. All that stuff about blasting rocks and highwaymen was just lies. But we've been summoned to a county court this autumn. I as a defendant and you as a witness to the fight.

HUNTER: Did you give him our names then?

WANDERER: No, I made two up on the spur of the moment.

HUNTER: Why? Now they can sue us for falsification as well. Fancy messing things up like that! What's my name supposed to be then?

WANDERER: I said you were travelling under the name of Incognito. And the peasants believed me.

HUNTER: And now I have to testify against you?

WANDERER: In three months' time, yes. In the meantime, let's make the most of our freedom and move on. I've heard there's a fair going on in the next village.

HUNTER: What sort of a fair?

WANDERER: A kind of *jeux floraux* or a donkeys' fête, where the village ass will be crowned with gold paper.

HUNTER: That sounds fun. What's the name of the village?

WANDERER: It's called Eselsdorf. And this one is called Lügenwald because it's full of liars.

HUNTER: "*Entevten exelavneir*", and on they marched . . .

WANDERER: . . . "*parasangas treis*", three parasangs . . .

HUNTER: . . . and so be it!

SCENE THREE

In Eselsdorf.

Eselsdorf. To the left a smithy, to the right a bench where the Hunter and the Wanderer are sitting.

HUNTER: We've been travelling together for some time now . . .

WANDERER: . . . without getting any closer. I don't even know what you do for a living.

HUNTER: I'm a soldier. I told you. I'm always fighting . . . fighting to keep my integrity . . .

WANDERER: But you're not always successful.

HUNTER: That would be asking too much . . .

WANDERER: . . . especially as we learn more from defeats.

HUNTER: Especially other people's defeats, you mean.

WANDERER: But the terrible thing is that you don't always know
who's won, because in the last war it was the winning
nation that suffered the greatest losses.

HUNTER: Which war?

WANDERER: The one at the windmills.

HUNTER: May I borrow your pen-knife. I've lost mine in the
mountains.

WANDERER: We mustn't be too inquisitive, but if you look closely at
this knife you'll find that it reveals quite a lot. The big
blade has hardly been used . . . which indicates that the
owner hasn't used his knife in a professional capacity;
the small blade on the other hand, shows traces of lead
and coloured crayons . . . so it might belong to an
artist, but it could be an amateur artist of course; the
cork-screw is well utilized which points to a keen beer-
drinker; here we've got a drill and a saw and this is a
picklock . . . that's ominous . . . but it's only been
thrown in as an extra. So we didn't learn very much
after all.

HUNTER: I see . . . this is Eselsdorf! And here is our
schoolmaster. This time we must keep our mouths shut
or we'll get mixed up again.

WANDERER: I wonder if that will help.

SCHOOL-
MASTER: *(Enters)* Abra-cadabra, abracadabra, ab-ra-ca-dab-ra!
(Looks at the strangers.) No! They didn't hear. Once
again: Abra-ca-dabra, abra-cadabra, abra-ca-da-bra.
No, these toffee-nosed people know how to restrain
themselves. Gentlemen, he who doesn't venture an
opinion must be presumed to agree with me. Will you
accept a challenge from the most prominent intellectual
individuals of this village? They'd like to challenge you
both to a verbal duel. If I don't get a response I
presume the answer to be in the affirmative. One, two,
three.

HUNTER AND
WANDERER: No!

SCHOOL-
MASTER: Good.

WANDERER: You are not so stupid considering you're from
Eselsdorf.

SCHOOL-
MASTER: I'm the only sane person in this village. That's why I
have to play the fool – to avoid being locked up. I have
an academic education; I have written a tragedy in five
acts, a verse drama. It's called 'Potamogeton'. It's so
damn stupid that I ought to have won the first prize
for it but the local blacksmith surpassed me in stupidity
and submitted a homage to the Destroyer of the
Country, so I didn't get a prize after all. They ignore me,
you see. You probably think I'm selfish talking about
myself, but I have two reasons for this. Firstly, I have
to introduce myself to you, secondly you wouldn't be
too pleased if I talked about you, would you now? Here
is the blacksmith. I'd better put on my disguise or he'll
think I'm perfectly normal and then he'll have me
locked up.

Puts his asses' ears on.

BLACKSMITH: *(Enters)* Abra-ca-da-bra, abra-cadabra.

SCHOOL-
MASTER: Neither rhyme nor reason.

BLACKSMITH: Are you making fun of me?

SCHOOL-
MASTER: Life is a battle and we're all soldiering on.

BLACKSMITH: Are you referring to the issue of women's emancipation
or the question of free trade?

SCHOOL-
MASTER: Two times two make four and six more make eight. Do
you get it?

BLACKSMITH: I reserve the exclusive rights to the subject of
arithmetics . . . because that is my chief subject after
'*quattuor species*' . . . *id est* the four rules of arithmetic

in whole numbers, including fractions, except ordinary
whole fractions and decimal fractions.

SCHOOL-
MASTER: Sometimes even Homer goes to sleep . . .

BLACKSMITH: But six and four make eleven and if you move the
comma two steps to the left, it will be as straight as a
nail. Isn't that right, gentlemen? Am I not right?

WANDERER: Quite right. Six and four make eleven, not eight.

BLACKSMITH: Now let's move on to some lighter ingredients, i.e.
topics of conversation. A topic, gentlemen, is not
something you blow out of your nose so to speak, if
you pardon the expression, not even when the topic is
of the light-weight variety. A light topic can be divided
into two equal parts; at close inspection, the first is the
subject *per se* . . . everything has a subject after all . . .
then follows the conversation. The subjects can be as
numerous as the days in a year, or more even . . . the
drops in the ocean . . . or let's say the sand granules in
the desert. I've never been in a desert, mind you, but I
can easily imagine how it might look. I've been on a
steamer once, though. It was an expensive trip I can
assure you . . . in case you didn't know . . . but now to
the point . . .

SCHOOL-
MASTER: The Guano Islands are situated on the 56th longitude
and the 13th latitude . . . east, south-east.

BLACKSMITH: Are you pulling my leg? I don't like people pulling my
leg.

SCHOOL-
MASTER: But that's not a patch on Charlemagne.

BLACKSMITH: No, but it's harder to shoe an ambler to prevent him
from wearing down his heels.

SCHOOL-
MASTER: As Hafir so rightly puts it in the third sura, pagina 78.
"Eat, man. You don't know when you'll be granted
another life again".

BLACKSMITH: I just want to point out that it's called pagina, like in Karolina etc. Isn't that right? Isn't it called pagina?

SCHOOL-
MASTER: Yes, yes, yes.

BLACKSMITH: Yes, we must get it right . . . on principle. . . . Do you know when Julius Caesar was born? *(To the others.)* I bet he doesn't.

SCHOOL-
MASTER: Julius Caesar was born in the year 99 before Christ.

BLACKSMITH: Before Christ? That is impossible. We started our calendar in the year one, and we don't count backwards now, do we?

SCHOOL-
MASTER: Don't we count backwards?

BLACKSMITH: Don't you try it with me! You better be careful! You've got such a weak head you never know what might happen to it. Do you know the difference between rye and wheat?

SCHOOL-
MASTER: Julius Caesar was born in 99 and he died in 31 . . .

BLACKSMITH: Did you hear that? How is that? Do you mean that he lived backwards? – The difference between rye and wheat is . . . well, first there's a difference in price, secondly there's the toll tax. Rye has a protective duty levied on it and wheat doesn't. Isn't that right?

SCHOOL-
MASTER: Yes, yes, yes.

BLACKSMITH: But the standard of currency is a different matter. I'm a silver man. I make no bones about it and the money exchange . . . that's a different matter too, and the exchange rates is something else again, so is 'agio'.

SCHOOL-
MASTER: What's that?

BLACKSMITH: What's that! Do I have to tell you that? Don't you think I've got better things to do? Haven't I paid my contribution, am I not married? I only ask . . . only ask. If any of you has any objection I'd like to have a

word with you in private, in private. Do you know
what that means? Behind the stables. I don't want a
word from you. I don't like being contradicted. No
one must contradict me. Do you consider the matter
closed – in my favour? Or shall we go behind the
stables? I'm a very serious man, not to be trifled with.
Now, gentlemen, you can see what kind of an ass
you're facing. I'm not referring to myself of course –
but the schoolmaster who claims that it's possible to be
born before the year one. But I'm going to tell you
what sort of a man he is. He is the stupidest creature
who's ever trodden this earth. He is so stupid that he
believes there is such a thing as the Guano Islands!
There's no such thing. *(Takes out a bottle and drinks
from it.)* And he doesn't know the difference between
rye and wheat – and he's a tippler – perhaps you think
that I drink too much as well but I just uncork a few
bottles now and again. That can hardly be called
drinking . . . no, that's something else. Knowledge,
gentlemen, is a virtue, but the schoolmaster knows
nothing, absolutely nothing and he is supposed to
educate our children; he's a tyrant too, a power-hungry
poor wretch and a fighter, so now you know what sort
of a man you're facing.

WANDERER: Wait a minute! I'm not going to dispute that . . .
because I don't want to pick a fight. I'm not going to
ask any questions either because I'm sure that would
just reveal your ignorance. And I'm not going to offer
you a drink because I don't think you need one. Nor
am I going to argue with you, because you'd never
understand what I mean, anyway . . . and you'd never
admit that I was right . . . but I would like to ask you
one question.

BLACKSMITH: Ask away, but ask nicely!

WANDERER: You're a man of character, isn't that right?

BLACKSMITH: I'm a man of real character, yes. Strong of character in
other words.

WANDERER: And you're a silver man?

BLACKSMITH: I'm proud to be called a silver man.

WANDERER :   You don't acknowledge gold as a standard of value in
              world trade?

BLACKSMITH : No, I do not.

WANDERER :   Not even for private use?

BLACKSMITH : Let me think. *(Aside)* Maybe this is a trick. *(Aloud)* I
             won't answer that question. I don't want to answer it
             . . . and no one can force me to answer. There is
             nothing wrong with my brain . . . but I can't
             understand the question.

WANDERER :   Can't you? Perhaps you were worried that your strong
              character might let you down when put to the test?

BLACKSMITH : Are you mocking me? You'd better not, you know,
             because I rule supreme in this village. I'm despotic!

              Wanderer laughs.

              Don't look at me like that. I'm a terrible despot.

WANDERER :   I wasn't looking at you. I was just laughing.

BLACKSMITH : Don't laugh. I pay 1500 shillings a year to vote for the
             local council . . . and that's no laughing matter. I have
             five children . . . all well brought up . . . richly
             endowed by nature . . . especially as far as their brains
             are concerned . . . but two are in America, I'm afraid.
             These things happen, and one of them has committed a
             crime . . . but he's had his punishment, so it's not
             worth talking about. No, not at all.

WANDERER :   *(Aside)* He beats the rest of the villagers by a long
              chalk.

HUNTER :   I can't listen to him for much longer. He makes me
              choke . . .

BLACKSMITH : I'm just going to get my manuscript and then we can
             start the celebrations. You mustn't leave
             meanwhile. . . . I am the Mayor and I want to be
             obeyed. The school-master has promised to read for us
             from his tragedy 'Potomogeton', It's not a bad play,
             considering it's written by an amateur, but many dogs
             are the death of one hare, as they say.

SCHOOL-
MASTER :   And the stanzas run by themselves, like strapping
                goslings.

BLACKSMITH : Are you making fun of me?

SCHOOL-
MASTER :   Surely not. You're a full-grown man, aren't you?

BLACKSMITH : Full-fledged is the word we use about birds. Read
                nicely for these gentlemen and I'll be back in a minute.
                But I don't want you to talk about me as soon as my
                back is turned.

WANDERER :   It would be harder while you're still here.

BLACKSMITH : You've got a point there. And if you have to choose
                between two evils, you pick the better of the two, don't
                you? *Ergo*: Talk about me behind my back.

                    Exits.

WANDERER :   What kind of a place is this? Is it a lunatic asylum or
                something?

SCHOOL
MASTER :   Yes, their wickedness has made them mad.

WANDERER :   Are you under guard?

SCHOOL-
MASTER :   I am under observation; I am suspected of being sane,
                you see.

WANDERER :   Come with us then. Let's run away together.

SCHOOL-
MASTER :   Then they'll round us all up.

WANDERER :   So they're not just stupid then.

SCHOOL-
MASTER :   Evil is both the mother and offspring of madness.

WANDERER :   Who is this blacksmith fellow?

SCHOOL-
MASTER :   He is the Beelzebub that Isaiah talks about. He is made
                up of other people's wickedness, envy and hatred and
                lies. He was appointed Mayor because the baker was
                the worthiest candidate; when I had served the town

faithfully for twenty-five years they gave a party for the blacksmith. At the last asses' festival the blacksmith received the laurel wreath because he had written the worst piece of poetry.

HUNTER: I prefer flight to a poor fight. We can't fight this one so let's flee instead.

WANDERER: Our lives are in danger here.

SCHOOL-
MASTER: But running away would be even more dangerous.

WANDERER: Can't we outwit them if they're so stupid?

SCHOOL-
MASTER: But they are shrewd like all stupid people.

WANDERER: Let's try! Mr Blacksmith . . . I say . . .

            Blacksmith leaves.

            Abra-cadabra, abra-cadabra.

BLACKSMITH: *(Re-enters)* What do you want? Are you leaving? Please don't. Please, don't do that.

WANDERER: We're just off to the next village to fetch some things for the fête.

BLACKSMITH: What are you going to fetch?

WANDERER: Props.

BLACKSMITH: I suppose you mean proper things. Yes, they're always welcome. Especially if they're made of iron.

WANDERER: They consist of shoenails, rifles, scythes and spades.

BLACKSMITH: Excellent.

WANDERER: But we want the schoolmaster to help us with the carrying . . .

BLACKSMITH: He's got no strength in his arms. Besides, he is so stupid.

WANDERER: The props will prop him up.

BLACKSMITH: True, true. But rifles are heavy things and require strong muscles.

WANDERER: On the other hand, rifles are hardly to be used as props.

BLACKSMITH: True, true, Off you go then. But make sure you return safely.

WANDERER: Don't you realise one always returns to the point where one started.

BLACKSMITH: I know something that keeps running away without ever coming back . . . something that ticks away without getting anywhere, in fact.

WANDERER: The clock, you mean. But we are not clocks so you can rest assured . . . we'll be back.

BLACKSMITH: That's logical enough, I suppose. But wait a minute! Do you mean to say that you will return without your clocks then?

WANDERER: They are not clocks. They are called watches.

BLACKSMITH: Very true, clocks are bigger things altogether. And they chime. . . . But wait a minute . . . clocks don't run away, do they? *Ergo* . . .

WANDERER: We're leaving now, and that's the main thing.

BLACKSMITH: Quite so. That's the main thing. And it's logical to boot. I like logical reasoning in all circumstances and I'm only able to follow a discussion if it's strictly logical.

WANDERER: A good enough reason for not following us, because we're not a strictly logical discussion.

BLACKSMITH: Quite right. Consequently, I'll stay behind. You go without me. Off you go . . .

WANDERER: Here's a song of praise to the ass, great wordsmith!
"The cleverest of all God's creatures . . .
your hearing is most acute
because your long ear is like a horn
you can hear the grass grow under the stones
and you're able to look to the east and the west . . .
at the same time.
I can read your character in your stiff legs
your strong will is a law unto itself . . .
when you're asked to stand still you prefer to run

and when your master uses the whip to make you stir you stubbornly refuse to move".

BLACKSMITH: That sums it up very well . . . because the mammal in question has been neglected long enough. No one has spoken up for it and it really was in need of rehabili . . .

WANDERER: . . . tation. But have you ever heard a dumb donkey speak?

BLACKSMITH: No, but that's beside the point. What matters is the character, the strength of character and that's where I sympathize with the poor animal. I sympathize wholeheartedly with him. Yes, I do, I do.

WANDERER: Do you stick to that?

BLACKSMITH: Yes, I do.

WANDERER: Let's go then.

BLACKSMITH: Wait a minute! I stick to . . . but I'm not alone. My views are shared by all right-thinking, enlightened well-guided people. In one word: the nation gathers round my banner and when I stick to my guns, I can show you that you're wrong because right will be right. Isn't that logical?

SCHOOL-
MASTER: The highest right – is the highest wrong.

BLACKSMITH: And the people's voice is God's voice. Come here, good folk. Gather round . . . nation!

The 'people' enter: a few persons only.

WANDERER: Here's the nation, but there aren't very many of them.

BLACKSMITH: They may be few in numbers, but you have to visualize the rank and file behind them.

WANDERER: I can't see any.

BLACKSMITH: You can't see them for the simple reason that they are invisible. That's logical. Listen everybody: these learned charlatans claim that there is something called the Guano Islands. Surely you don't believe that there is such a thing, do you?

PEOPLE: No.

BLACKSMITH: So these gentlemen must be liars or else they are fools. Do we have a punishment severe enough for rascals who spread lies like that?

WANDERER: Yes, the severest punishment is to be forced into exile.

BLACKSMITH: Not bad. But we must have enough evidence first. Someone just said that Homer is asleep.

WANDERER: Sometimes.

BLACKSMITH: . . . sometimes . . . or always . . . and all the time. That's all one and the same. Sophistry, that's all. *(Addresses the people.)* Do you believe that a poet can be asleep . . . have you ever heard anything more ridiculous?

ONE OF THE
PEOPLE: Surely he must have slept at night.

BLACKSMITH: At night! Is that meant to be an answer? Have I given anyone here permission to answer? Come behind the stable barn with me and I'll give you a proper answer.

ONE OF THE
PEOPLE: Is this a question of taking sides?

BLACKSMITH: Yes, you should always take sides. Otherwise we don't know where you stand.

SCHOOL-
MASTER: *(To the Blacksmith.)* Why don't you read for us from your 'Charlemagne'! That'll put an end to this prattle. Our friends are in a hurry, you see. *(Aside to the Hunter and the Wanderer.)* It's not called Charlemagne but we'd better call it that or he may lock us up.

BLACKSMITH: I heard what you said. And I saw you making faces and it's a well-known fact that those who make faces are in collusion. Lock them up. You know what I mean. Have them arrested. He is not called Charlemagne, but that's what we call him. Because he was BIG you see. Cover their mouths and lock them up until they've retracted.

> *The Hunter, Wanderer and Schoolmaster are seized and are about to be led away.*

HUNTER :   But we've been banished from this village already and
                we were just about to set off for some props . . .

BLACKSMITH : That's true. That's quite true. I'll let you go but you
                must promise to come back and you must also promise
                to be grateful because an ungrateful person is the
                heaviest burden on earth . . . I have a wife . . . who
                keeps a salon. It may sound a little silly to you but she
                keeps a literary salon and I expect to see you both there
                when I send for you.

WANDERER :   So we're free. But at what price?

HUNTER :   Is it called freedom to be tied by a word of honour to
                an anchor chain in a literary salon?

BLACKSMITH : Get out of here, you two! But the nation . . . can stay.

Hunter, Wanderer and Schoolmaster leave.

SCENE FOUR

A shopping arcade in town.

*A number of shop-fronts on the right: a café, a photographer's, a shop
which sells shells; on the left, a shop which sells flowers and fruit, next a
Japanese tea and perfumery shop.*

The Hunter and the Wanderer are sitting outside the florist's shop.

WANDERER :   You look rather gloomy.

HUNTER :   The effect of this place.

WANDERER :   You've been here before?

HUNTER :   Yes, I used to live here.

WANDERER :   I could tell.

HUNTER :   We must find some chloroform . . . my wounds are
                beginning to ache.

WANDERER :   "*Vinum et circenes*". I bet we'll have some free
                entertainment here soon. This is the sewer of the town.
                Everything is channelled through this arcade. *(Beckons
                to someone in the restaurant; a waitress appears and puts
                a bottle of wine on the table.)* I suppose people will
                recognize you?

HUNTER: Impossible. I've grown a beard since I was here last, and this morning I had a hair-cut and washed my hands. No one in this town recognizes you if you've had a wash.

WANDERER: The waitress is looking at you.

HUNTER: Perhaps I remind her of an old friend.

WANDERER: What did I say? We've got some entertainment . . .

An organ grinder and his monkey enter.

WANDERER: Come here. Do us a favour will you . . . spare our poor heads for a small payment.

ORGAN
GRINDER: Heads?

WANDERER: Well, ears then, if you prefer. I'll give you a sovereign if you keep quiet

ORGAN
GRINDER: But people pay to see the monkey, not me.

WANDERER: Then we'll watch him do his tricks, but no musical accompaniment, please.

ORGAN
GRINDER: Don't you want to hear the words . . .

WANDERER: Is it true that people in this town are descended from apes?

ORGAN
GRINDER: That's right. You'd better show some respect for him . . .

WANDERER: Now I can see the resemblance . . . Yes. . . . By Jove, it's true. Let's have a look at the words then. That monster looks more like a goat than anything else.

ORGAN
GRINDER: Well, maybe you're right. Yes, maybe you are.

WANDERER: Do you really believe that that mammal in the scarlet coat . . . with a pistol in his hand has fathered the human race?

ORGAN
GRINDER: Do I detect a free-thinker in you, sir? In that case

you'd better be careful . . . We are orthodox in this town . . . we defend our faith.

WANDERER: Which faith?

ORGAN
GRINDER: The true faith, of course. We believe in The Descent of Man.

*

HUNTER: I suppose we might even be sued for blasphemy then. *(To the Wanderer.)* Where did the schoolmaster disappear to?

WANDERER: He vanished as soon as he had made use of us, of course.

HUNTER: Shall we move on?

WANDERER: What's the point? It's all the same if we get arrested here or somewhere else.

HUNTER: People are squatting like robbers in the ditches. Look into the café over there . . . the girl is staring at you with lowered eyelids as if begging you to take pity on her. She's beautiful . . . she's definitely capable of arousing other feelings than pity. Supposing you wanted to save her from her rather humiliating existence in there; supposing you decided to invite her home, and protect her from the worst misfortunes in life. What would happen, do you think? She'd soon rob you of your friends, your family, your colleagues, and your benefactors. In a word, she'd devour you.

WANDERER: What if I wouldn't let her? I suppose she'd sue me for maltreatment?

HUNTER: And accuse you of having ruined her youth . . . but the worst thing is that you'd become part of a family you don't even know . . .

WANDERER: But which I have my misgivings about . . . She is pulling and drawing me in there . . . stirring up a whirlpool, spinning a net which feels like warm air. . . . I'll go and tear it apart.

HUNTER: You may get caught up in it instead.

The Wanderer walks into the café.

HUNTER: *(Alone)* One man gone to the dogs . . .

                              ⋆

PHOTOGRA-
PHER: *(Enters with a camera.)* May I take a portrait of you,
            sir?

HUNTER: No.

PHOTOGRA-
PHER: Please, I am a poor man.

HUNTER: Alright then, but you mustn't put the picture on
            display, either on cigarette packets or soap wrappers;
            and if I end up looking like an Aboriginal or a mass
            murderer you must promise me to throw the negative
            away.

PHOTOGRA-
PHER: You are so suspicious, sir.

HUNTER: Not at all, I am just cautious.

            *The Photographer waves in the direction of his shop;
            his wife comes out.*

                              ⋆

PHOTOGRA-
PHER: May I introduce my wife . . . she usually helps me with
            the developing. Come here, Euphrosyne. I've promised
            to take this gentleman's picture, even though I'm very
            busy at the moment. Come here, Euphrosyne, converse
            with this gentleman while I get ready.

EUPHROSYNE:*(Sits down.)* You are a lucky man, sir, finding an artist
            like my husband. He is the cleverest man I know. If
            this picture doesn't turn out well it won't be his fault.
            You're a lucky man having your picture taken by him.
            We're doing you a favour.

HUNTER: Just a minute . . .

EUPHROSYNE:Yes, there is no need to be so high and mighty. You
            should be grateful that I ask you for a favour.

HUNTER: Wait a minute . . .

PHOTOGRA-
PHER: *(Calling)* Gotthard! Come here, you have put the plates
                back to front in the slide.

GOTTHARD: *(Entering)* I haven't put any plates in at all . . .

EUPHROSYNE: Is that a way to answer your father, your own father?

GOTTHARD: I don't know what you mean. I only handle shells.

PHOTOGRA-
PHER: You're handling them, you say . . . Yes. But are you
                selling any? Ask this gentleman if he needs any shells. I
                thought he mentioned something about shells just now
                . . .

HUNTER: I haven't said anything about shells. I just talked about
                cigarette packets and soap wrappers . . . that's all.

EUPHROSYNE: Gotthard, bring some cigarettes, will you? Didn't you
                hear that the gentleman wants some?

HUNTER: I just said I didn't want my picture on soap wrappers.

GOTTHARD: *(Sits down.)* You're difficult to please, sir. I realise that
                now. But let's talk it through and try and solve this
                problem . . .

EUPHROSYNE: You're right, Gotthard, this gentleman must be put in
                the picture, so to speak. Ask Klara to come out . . .

GOTTHARD: *(Calls)* Klara!

★

Klara, the florist, enters.

EUPHROSYNE: Try selling some flowers to this gentleman. He is so
                mean he doesn't even want to buy a shell . . . even
                though Gotthard has the most beautiful shells.

KLARA: *(Sits down.)* Maybe it's possible to exchange a few
                words with him . . . but he looks rather toffee-nosed,
                doesn't he? Is he a hunter?

EUPHROSYNE: Can't you tell?

KLARA: So he kills animals. You mustn't do that. That's a sin.
                But he looks cruel too, like all drunkards. Yes, those
                who drink before noon are drunkards . . .

HUNTER: *(To Klara.)* What have you done with your husband?
          (Klara is frightened.) It's a sin to kill people, didn't you
          know?

KLARA: What do you mean?

HUNTER: I mean . . .

KLARA: Did you hear that, everybody? He means . . .

ALL: Yes, we heard.

HUNTER: Let me just say something. Just one word.

GOTTHARD: No. Why should you?

HUNTER: It's not what you think I'm going to say. It's something
          quite different.

EUPHROSYNE:*(Curious)* Let's hear it then.

HUNTER: Is Möller arrested yet?

          Everybody rises in horror.

                              *

WANDERER: *(From the café.)* What's the matter now?

HUNTER: Is Möller arrested yet? *(They all disperse with
          threatening gestures.)* For the third time: Is Möller
          arrested?

          They all leave.

                              *

WANDERER: What was that supposed to mean?

HUNTER: That was the village secret. Everybody knows that
          Möller is a murderer, but no one dares give evidence
          against him, because they lack proof. The result of my
          bombshell will be that we'll have to leave. Come on.

WANDERER: I can't.

HUNTER: Stuck?

WANDERER: In an ale-house . . . dregs in the glasses . . . spent
          matches . . . cigar ash . . . there she is . . . pawed by
          various young gentlemen . . . enveloped in smoke, and
          with dark rings under her eyes, and yet, yet, I'm
          ensnared . . .

HUNTER: Break loose.

WANDERER: I can't.

HUNTER: Let's run away.

WANDERER: I can't.

HUNTER: Well, stay here then.

WANDERER: I can't. I can't do anything.

HUNTER: I'll say goodbye.

WANDERER: We'll meet again.

HUNTER: One always does . . .

WANDERER: Goodbye.

              Goes into the café.

                              ★

HUNTER: (*Alone, paces up and down in the shopping arcade, stops
             in front of the photographer's camera.*) This belonged to
             me once . . . a long time ago. I used to walk here under
             the glass roof when it rained . . . when my mind was
             troubled . . . there were always candles burning in here
             . . . and flowers and fruit to please the eye . . . and the
             shells that whispered fairy tales from the sea . . .
             Here are pictures of some acquaintances . . . or semi-
             acquaintances; they helped me pass the time when I
             was on my own.
             A look, a facial expression was enough for me to feel
             kinship with someone . . . they're still here. This is my
             oldest friend; he's probably got grey hairs by now, but
             . . . his picture has turned yellow like an autumn leaf . . .
             Here are relatives and ex-relatives, a brother-in-law
             who is not my brother-in-law any more. And here . . .
             Oh, Good Lord, help me. My child! My child which
             isn't mine . . . has been, but is no more. Someone
             else's. And yet mine.
             And this was my café. Our table. A long time ago,
             all this has ceased to be, but it lives on in memory.
             The fire which cannot be put out, which burns but
             doesn't warm, which burns but doesn't consume.

*

*An old Japanese man enters from the tea shop. He
looks a dying man. The Hunter goes up to him and
supports him with his arm.*

JAPANESE: At last – a human being. Where did you come from?
            And where are you going?

HUNTER: From the great highway. What can I do for you?

JAPANESE: Help me to die.

HUNTER: There'll be time for that soon enough.

JAPANESE: I can't live any longer . . . I have no one to turn to for
            the last favour, there is not a single human being in
            this town who . . .

HUNTER: What last favour do you mean?

JAPANESE: I want you to hold my sword while I . . .

HUNTER: I can't do that. Why do you have to die anyway?

JAPANESE: Because I can't live any more.

HUNTER: Tell me your story then. But be brief.

JAPANESE: Yes. Yes.
            I left my country because I had committed a crime, you
            see. I came here determined to become an honest
            person – and observe the laws of conscience and
            honour. I sold decent goods for a reasonable price, but
            people only like *fakes* . . . and they must be cheap. So I
            had no alternative. . . . Instead of distilling the scent
            from the flowers, I gave them chemical substances, and
            instead of tea leaves I gave them leaves from the sloe
            bush and the cherry tree. At first my conscience didn't
            trouble me. I had to make a living after all. But one
            day fifteen years ago, it was as if everything I had ever
            done in my life was written down in a book . . . and
            the book lay open before me. Day and night, night and
            day I read all the false columns, all the irregularities I'd
            entered. And I've struggled, but in vain. Only death
            can release me from my torment because most of the
            evil is in the flesh; my soul has been cleansed through
            suffering.

HUNTER: In what way can I help you?

JAPANESE: This! I'll take a sleeping draught and you'll put me in a coffin and take it to the crematorium . . .

HUNTER: What if you wake up before we get there?

JAPANESE: I've thought of that too. I want to be conscious when it happens so I can feel the cleansing power of the fire for a short moment . . . suffer . . . and then the liberating bliss.

HUNTER: And afterwards?

JAPANESE: I want you to collect my ashes and put them in my most precious vase . . .

HUNTER: And inscribe your name on it? What is your name, by the way?

JAPANESE: Just a minute . . . I have lived, erred and suffered under the name of Hiroshima, the town of my birth. But in my country we have a custom . . . when a person dies he abandons his old name and gets a new one, which we call the eternal name. That's the only name I want on my tombstone, plus a maxim, but before that I want you to sacrifice a branch of the sakaki tree . . . when I'm dead.

HUNTER: Have you prepared all these things?

JAPANESE: Yes. Look here.

HUNTER: What does this name mean?

JAPANESE: "*Harahara to*". It means: 'Rustling leaves' or 'crisp silk', but it also means 'falling tears'.

HUNTER: And the maxim?

JAPANESE:

> Chiru hana wo
> nanika uramin
> Yo no naka ni
> waga ni tomo ni
> aramu no kawa

HUNTER: Which means?

JAPANESE:

> 'Distracted flowers
> why am I angry

Even I – with the others
must perish according to the will of the gods'.

HUNTER: I shall do what you ask of me. But don't you have any next of kin?

JAPANESE: I did have. I had a daughter who came here three years ago when she thought I was dying. She came hoping to inherit from me, but when I didn't die she got angry – couldn't conceal her feelings – and left again. After that she was dead to me.

HUNTER: And where is this supposed to take place . . . this . . . thing . . . we've just been talking about?

JAPANESE: Outside the town, by the crematorium.

HUNTER: Shall we make our way there together or do you prefer us to meet there?

JAPANESE: Let us meet in the bower of the resting-place . . . in a little while. I just want to shave and have a bath first . . .

HUNTER: Fine. Let's meet there then.

JAPANESE: *(Goes back to his shop nodding to himself.)* Here comes the murderer. Be careful.

HUNTER: Is it him?

JAPANESE: Be careful. He is the most powerful man in town.
  Leaves.

*

MÖLLER: *(Enters, stiffly; proud but with floppy, somewhat awkward arm movements. Stares at Hunter.)* Isn't it . . .

HUNTER: No, it isn't.

MÖLLER: I see. Then it must be . . .

HUNTER: No, it used to be . . . the one you're thinking about isn't alive any more . . .

MÖLLER: You're dead in other words?

HUNTER: Yes. Twelve years ago I committed hara-kiri; I killed my old self. The person you see here before you is a total stranger to you and will remain so.

MÖLLER: I remember now. You were foolish enough to confess all your sins and weaknesses in public.

HUNTER: And everyone loved it. They all felt so much better for .my revelations. No one sympathised . . . or approved of my confession.

MÖLLER: No, why should they?

HUNTER: But when, after ten years of suffering . . . I had atoned for my sins and put things right again, I decided to reveal your sins as well. But that didn't go down too well . . .

MÖLLER: Well, what do you expect for Chrissake.

HUNTER: You, for instance, who are guilty of murder . . .

MÖLLER: We don't use that word . . . especially when there's no proof . . .

HUNTER: I know you are a powerful man these days; you tyrannize the duke himself . . . thanks to the existence of some freemasonry . . .

MÖLLER: What's that?

HUNTER: You know. An alliance – which is not exactly holy . . .

MÖLLER: What about you?

HUNTER: I've never belonged to it . . . but I recognize certain signs . . .

MÖLLER: Look into the shop window over there and you'll see who you are.

HUNTER: You mean that caricature? That's not me. That's you. That's how you look inside. It's your creation. You're welcome to it.

MÖLLER: You're clever at getting rid of your own vermin.

HUNTER: Why don't you do the same? But do it the way I did, and keep your distance from me. Put your head on the chopping block like I did, like I had to do when you made me into your scapegoat and heaped all your sins upon me.

MÖLLER: What do you want?

HUNTER: For instance. . . . Somebody once wrote this bit of nonsense . . . that if he stood alone on Gaurisankar and the Flood were to come and drown the whole human race, it didn't matter as long as he survived. Do you know who the author was? – At the next carnival Gaurisankar was carried in the procession and at the top was an effigy of me, not the author. What do you say to that? And when it was my birthday he was honoured. – And when I had invented those new insulators, you got the prize, remember. But when you had committed a murder, the accusing finger pointed at me. And when the price of sugar rose on the stock market, people blamed it on my insulators . . . the insulators that you'd been awarded a prize for. Have you ever heard of anything more absurd? Doubly absurd, like standing on your head while turning back to front.

MÖLLER: Do you have any evidence?

HUNTER: Yes, I do.

     Möller is amazed.

     But I don't have the courage to present it in front of a jury consisting of your friends, because they would deny the facts put before them and have me arrested instead. Who is the girl in there by the way . . . the one who trapped my friend?

MÖLLER: It is . . . your daughter.

HUNTER: *(His hand to his heart. Suddenly white-faced, and when he holds his handkerchief to his mouth it reddens with blood.)* The child whom you've brought up. *(Short pause.)* I'm going to the crematorium now.

     Exits.

SCENE FIVE

In the park outside the crematorium.

An avenue of cypresses, a bench, a chair, a table.

HUNTER: *(Enters alone.)*
               What's this? A collection of urns,
               but all alike?
               A pharmacy, a museum? No!
               A dove-cote, a house of pigeons . . .
               but there are no doves . . . no olive branch . . .
               just husks; the wheat is growing elsewhere;
               in urns and boxes, identical like dust and dust . . .
               these have all been human beings once . . .
               now they're labelled and numbered . . .
               "Here rests" . . . I knew you,
               but you never got to know yourself . . .
               and you . . . you always walked around in disguise,
               all your long, hard-working life.
               And when I tore the mask, you died.
               'Idolater' was your name.
               We had to idolize your weird wife
               and your detestable children,
               if we hadn't, you would have sacrificed us,
               cut us up with a flint-knife one Saturday
               or lynched us in the Sunday tabloid . . .
               robbed us of bread and honour.

               Murderer (Möller) enters, listens.

               You shining torch of this town, you gathered the whole
               nation around your death bed;
               even when you were dead,
               you managed to count the wreaths
               and threatened to avenge yourself on those who hadn't
                   sent any.

MURDERER: It's beautiful by a graveside.

HUNTER: This isn't a grave, it's just a jar with some rubbish in it.
               No, a stone. You see, he turned into stone in the end.

MURDERER: Tell me something about yourself.

HUNTER: I spoke about myself thirteen years ago. Surely you
               heard enough then. But here are the ashes of someone
               I'd like to pay my respects to, except that he was
               murdered . . . by you.

He never hurt anyone on purpose, he only acted in
self-defence and when he refused to be your accomplice
you killed him but first you ruined him.

MURDERER: I hear you're meeting that crooked Japanese . . .

HUNTER: Are you going to interfere in my life like HE did?

MURDERER: Don't speak ill of the dead. You should say 'that poor
            man'.

HUNTER: That's what you always call criminals when they get
            their fingers stuck in the honey-pot . . . but never your
            victims . . . I want you to leave now . . . quickly.

MURDERER: I'll leave when I want to.

            *Hunter produces his bloody handkerchief and shows
            him. Murderer turns round and leaves.*

            I can't stand the sight of blood. It's just one of those
            things with me.

HUNTER: Since the fourth of April.

            Murderer withdraws.

            (To the Japanese.) Are you prepared for the journey
            now?

JAPANESE: I am, but let's sit down and wait
            while the oven is getting hot.

HUNTER: With pleasure. *(They sit down.)*
            Now that your life lies there at your feet
            like a head of game, hunted, shot and killed . . .
            how does it feel? Tell me.

JAPANESE: *(After a pause.)*
            It's like a line with many loops in it,
            like the doodles on a piece of blotting-paper,
            your hand-writing in reverse,
            but if you hold a mirror to it you can read it.

HUNTER: Which was the worst stumbling-block you came
            across?

JAPANESE:　　*(Thinks)*
I saved an enemy once . . .
and afterwards he stabbed me.
When you have to regret something good
that you've done, it's hard.
On another occasion I spoke well of an oppressed,
he turned against me . . . and robbed me of everything
and I was defenceless in an uneven battle,
because he had it in writing . . . from me
that he was superior as a person.
But all that is nothing,
nothing compared to life itself . . .
the humiliating experience of walking around
like a naked skeleton dressed in flesh
and set into motion by sinews and strings . . .
by a little motor in the engine room
of the chest, propelled by the heat
created by the carbohydrates in the stomach . . .
and the soul, the spirit perched in the heart,
like a bird in the rib-cage.
Little bird, I shall soon open the cage for you
and let you fly . . . home to your island
of flowers and sunshine,
where once I was born,
but where I wasn't allowed to die.
Look here! My best vase, my family heirloom
which will now hold the dust of a piece of dust . . .
but which used to contain flowers
on festive occasions . . . where young eyes
and red cheeks were reflected
in the gold-rimmed goblets . . .
and a little hand passed round the best
that the house could offer to the children.

But now you've become a flask of tears, dear vase
because all the good things life granted us
became objects of sorrow in the end.

I remember . . . it was around New Year . . .
when the children had their dolls' party . . .
we used to keep the dolls from one generation to the next.

A child!
What is more perfect of its kind

than this little creature?
Not a man, not a woman,
but both, yet neither . . .
a human being in miniature.

But I'm sorry, I have forgotten you
in my grief . . . tell me something
about yourself! Something about your life.
How do you see life now and how did you use to?
What did you find hardest, bitterest of all?

HUNTER: I found that more bitter than death . . . the fact
that we had to take this great mockery seriously . . .
that we had to hold sacred that which was so coarse.

When I joined in this ludicrous game
I ended up crying.
and when I too became coarse like the others,
I was made to feel ashamed.

And then . . . I was a bit of a preacher too.
At first I spoke well of mankind,
dwelled on the beauty I saw around me . . .
and had great aims in life,
what is commonly known as ideals . . .
bright flags on proud posts . . .
which attract people on holy days and festivals.
But now . . . how bitter . . . all the beautiful things
I have thought and spoken . . . I have to take it all back.
Beauty does not exist in life,
cannot be realised down here on earth . . .
the ideal does not come true.

JAPANESE: I know . . . but it is a memory,
a hope, a beacon to steer us . . .
and therefore: let's fill the place!
Let the flags billow out . . .
they are raised high and can be seen from afar . . .
and show the way up . . . towards the sun!

HUNTER: The oven is ready and glowing . . .

JAPANESE: Casting its red light on the crowns of the cypresses
like a rosy dawn when the sun is rising . . .
Welcome, day! Farewell, night,
with your heavy dreams.

For the last time I undress
and seek rest and fall asleep . . .

And when I wake up . . . I shall be with my mother,
my wife, my children and friends!
Good night, you poor human being.

Leaves.

*The stage is lit up and in the clouds we see the same
picture of "The Land of Wishes" as in the first scene.*

SCENE SIX

At the last gate.

*At the back two white gates open to a sandy beach and the blue sea. To
the left a red cottage surrounded by beeches. Left of that a hornbeam
hedge and an orchard. Outside the house to the left a table is laid for a
name's day party. Above the hornbeam hedge a shuttlecock keeps bouncing
up and down. A perambulator with a blue hood pulled up is standing
beside the gate.*

HUNTER: *(Enters, lost in thought.)*
               Alone!
               It is the end
               when you want to cling to life
               and not go bartering
               and hustle for a better position –
               when you won't be bought
               or put down any more . . .

               When I first realised –
               when the thought first struck me
               that I was shut up in a mad-house,
               a house of correction,
               I wanted to lose my senses
               so no one could guess what I thought . . .
               "Telo, Telo mananai!"
               I want to, I wanted to be mad!
               And wine became my faithful companion
               I hid under the veils of intoxication.
               People soon forgot who I was
               because of my clown's costume.
               Now things have changed

and the drink of oblivion
has turned into the drink of remembrance.
And I remember everything, everything.
The seals are broken, the books are revealed.
They read aloud to themselves
and when my ear is tired I see,
I see, see everything, everything!

Wakes up.

Where have I got to? The seaside?
And a beech forest, a forester's cabin
and over there, a shuttlecock that goes up and down.
A pram with a new-born babe in it
the little hood like the blue firmament
is arched above the innocent sleeping babe . . .
in the red house with the green shutters
there is a couple hiding
their happiness concealed . . .
because happiness does exist
but it is brief like lightning
like sunshine, like the convolvulus
which flowers for one day
and then no more!
There's smoke coming from the kitchen chimney,
the well-stocked larder at the back,
a small cellar below,
a light verandah facing the forest . . .
I know how it ought to be . . .
how it used to be . . .

And here is the table laid
for the little one's name's day!
An altar raised to childhood
to hope, and innocent joy . . .
founded on its own happiness . . .
not bought at other people's expense . . .
and there is the beach
with its white clean soft warm sand . . .
with its shells and pebbles
and blue water to paddle in . . .
in bare feet . . .
It is decorated with birch twigs and leaves
and the paths are freshly raked . . .

they must be expecting guests – a children's party.
The flowers have been watered . . .
the flowers of my childhood –
Wolf's bane with two doves in it
the emperor's crown with its tiara
and the sceptre, the apple.
The flower of passion . . . suffering
white and amethyst, with the cross
and the lance, the nails . . .
visited by a busy bee that extracts
honey from its cup . . .
where we find only gall . . .
and over there the most beautiful tree of all . . .
in the children's garden of Eden.
Through dark green leaves
the fair berries look out
with their red and white cherry-cheeks, two by two . . .
little children's faces – brother and sister
who play and hug each other
when they're rocked by the wind . . .
And between the branch and the trunk a garden warbler
has built his nest
the invisible singer, a song on wings
Shhh! The sand is crunching under a child's boots . . .
Here comes the empress!

*

CHILD: *(Enters, takes the Hunter's hand and guides him to the
             pram.)* Walk quietly and I'll show you my doll. –
             That's the doll. That's what we call her anyway. – But
             you mustn't walk on the path because it's just been
             raked. – Ellen has raked it because we're having visitors
             today. – It's my name's day, you see. – Are you sad?

HUNTER: What's your name, little one?

CHILD: My name is Maria.

HUNTER: Who lives in that house?

CHILD: Mummy and daddy.

HUNTER: Show me your name's day table.

CHILD: But we mustn't touch anything . . .

HUNTER: No, I'm not going to touch anything, little one. I
           promise.

CHILD: Do you know what we're having for dinner today?
           We're having asparagus and strawberries. Why are you
           so sad? Have you lost all your money? You can have
           one of the crackers on the table, but you mustn't have
           the big one because that's Stella's. Did you know Stella
           had bread crumbs in her bed last night and she cried
           and then there was a thunderstorm and then we got
           frightened and mummy shut the damper. She had a
           sandwich in her bed, you see and the sandwich broke
           because the bread was the sort that's made in town . . .
           the sort that breaks – like they buy in town – Shall we
           make up a story? Can you make up a story? What's
           your name?

HUNTER: I'm called . . . Karthafilos.

CHILD: No . . . you are not. . . .

HUNTER: Ahasverus then . . . who walks and walks . . .

CHILD: Let's talk about something else . . . do your eyes hurt?

HUNTER: Yes, they do, terribly terribly, my dear.

CHILD: You mustn't read by candlelight once you've gone to
           bed, because then your eyes will hurt.

           A bugle is heard.

CHILD: That's daddy!

           Exits.

HUNTER: My child! MY child!
           She didn't recognize me. Lucky . . .
           Lucky for us both.
           Farewell you lovely vision
           I don't want to stand in the way of the sun
           and shade the children's garden patch
           I know the father – and the mother too.
           A lovely parable that's slightly blurred,
           but beautiful all the same.
           A memory perhaps, or more than so:
           a hope – a summer's day in the forest
           by the sea – a name's day table and a cradle.

A ray of sunshine in a child's eyes
a gift from a little hand
and then onwards again and out . . . into the darkness.

SCENE SEVEN

The dark forest.

HUNTER: Alone! I've lost my way . . . in the dark!
"And Eliah sat down under a broom tree and prayed that he might die: I have had enough, Lord. Take my life."

VOICE: *(In the dark.)* "He that wants to lose his life shall find it".

HUNTER: Who is that speaking in the dark?

VOICE: Is it dark?

HUNTER: Is it dark?

WOMAN: *(Enters)* I asked, because I cannot see – I am blind, you see.

HUNTER: Have you always been blind?

WOMAN: No! When the tears stopped, my eyes couldn't see any more.

HUNTER: It's good to be able to cry.

WOMAN: But I can hear instead and I recognize your voice . . . I know who you are.
I believe in you, you know.

HUNTER: You mustn't believe in me, nor in other human beings. You must believe in God.

WOMAN: I do.

HUNTER: But God alone. Mankind is not worth believing in.

WOMAN: You used to defend good causes once upon a time?

HUNTER: I spoke up for the Only Truth, against idolaters . . . you were always so keen to idolize . . . yourselves, your relatives, your friends, but you never wanted to do justice to . . .

WOMAN: You sometimes abandoned your cause.

HUNTER: When I was tricked into feeling compassion for a
            wrongdoer, under the pretext that he'd been unfairly
            treated, I gave up fighting . . . an unjust cause . . .

WOMAN: You were also an evangelist once, but you grew tired of
            that too.

HUNTER: I didn't grow tired, but when I realised that I couldn't
            live as I preached I stopped preaching altogether
            because I didn't want to be branded a hypocrite. – And
            when I discovered that the beautiful doctrines couldn't
            be applied to real life I banished them to the Land of
            Fulfilled Wishes.

WOMAN: And now you are dead?

HUNTER: In a civil sense, yes, but spiritually no. I struggle,
            therefore I live. I don't exist, only what I've done
            exists. Good and bad . . . I've confessed and suffered
            for all the bad things I've done and I've tried to
            recompense good with good.

WOMAN: Do you still want to be a spokesman for mankind?

HUNTER: When they are right, otherwise no. I once spoke up for
            someone because I felt indebted to him in some way
            . . . but by doing so, I accidentally upset someone else.
            That's what happens with our noblest emotions. They
            often betray us.

WOMAN: You are accusing . . . you . . . the prosecutor.

HUNTER: Who am I accusing?

WOMAN: The 'management'.

HUNTER: Begone, Satan . . . before you tempt me to blaspheme.

WOMAN: Satan?

HUNTER: Yes, Satan.

WOMAN: No one was as black as you.

HUNTER: It was you who blackened me in your own image. But
            can you tell me why, when I confessed MY sins, YOU
            felt redeemed and thanked God that you were not like
            me, although you were every bit as bad. I once

witnessed an execution . . . when I was very young . . .
the crowd looked like a mob of hypocrites and when
they walked away from the place of execution they
pitied the poor man . . . but as soon as they got into
the tavern they bad-mouthed him. That made them feel
better than he. . . . But then some of them returned to
the Hanging Hill to collect a few drops of blood from
the dead man's body – a known cure for epilepsy –
they dipped their handkerchiefs in his blood; look at
this! Ah, you're blind. Touch it then. Your eye is in
your hand.

Hands over his bloody handkerchief.

WOMAN: It feels like red . . . but it's sticky . . . and it smells like
. . . at the butcher's. No, now I know. A relation of
mine died recently; first he coughed up his lungs and
then his heart.

HUNTER: Did he cough up his heart?

WOMAN: Yes, he did.

HUNTER: *(Looks at the handkerchief.)* I believe you. As I'm sure
you know, the goat is not a clean beast but on the great
day of atonement all the sins of mankind were heaped
upon him and thus he was driven into the desert to be
eaten by wild animals. That's the one we call the scapegoat.

WOMAN: Are you saying that you've been made to suffer for
other people's sins?

HUNTER: Both for my own and other people's, yes.

WOMAN: But before you defended just causes you had another
occupation?

HUNTER: Yes, I was an architect. I built many houses. They
weren't all good but whenever I did build something
really good, people didn't like it. So the work was
offered to others who were not as good. That happened
in the town of Thopheth where I built the theatre.

WOMAN: That is supposed to be a beautiful building.

HUNTER: Remember it then . . . when I am dead . . . and forget
me as a person.

WOMAN: "I do not exist, only the good that I have done exists. . . ." Why did you feel no compassion for your fellow human beings?

HUNTER: The question is incorrectly put. Have you ever met anyone who felt compassion for me? No. – How then do you expect me to return feelings which I have never been the recipient of? – And don't you remember who first said: "I feel sorry for humankind!"

Woman disappears.

★

HUNTER: She's gone. They always disappear . . . as soon as you try to defend yourself.

★

TEMPTER: *(Enters)* There you are! Now we're going to have a little talk, but it's a bit dark here so we're going to light some lovely candles . . . *(It gets lighter.)* so we can see each other – we need to see each other when we're going to talk sense. I've got greetings from the grand duke. He holds you in high esteem – he's offering you a position as court architect with a salary so and so, apartment with full board, heating included etc. You understand?

HUNTER: I don't want any position . . .

TEMPTER: Wait a minute. There's one condition. That is . . . well . . . in one word . . . you have to behave yourself. You have to behave like a normal human being.

HUNTER: I'd like to know how a normal human being behaves. Please tell me.

TEMPTER: Don't you know? Why do you look so distraught?

HUNTER: Why? I look distraught because I've had my head turned. I used to take people at face value; that's why I've been filled with lies. Everything that I used to believe in turned out to be lies. That's why I too am a fraud. I've roamed about with false opinions of people and life in general. I've worked with false premises, and passed counterfeit coins without knowing it. That's why I'm not the one I seem to be. I can't be with other

people, I can't speak, not even on someone else's
behalf, I can't appeal to a testimony without worrying
that it may be a lie. On several occasions, I've been an
accomplice in the anchor chain called society, but when
I started to resemble all the others, I decided to
become a man of the forest, a highwayman.

TEMPTER: That's just talk. Now let's return to the grand duke
who is asking for your services.

HUNTER: It is not my services he wants. He is after my soul . . .

TEMPTER: He wants you to show some interest in his big
enterprise . . .

HUNTER: I can't do that . . . go away now. I don't have long to
live and I want to be alone when I settle my
accounts . . .

TEMPTER: Ha! Ha! Is it time to pay the outstanding bills? In that
case, I shall present you with invoices, bills and suits . . .

HUNTER: Yes, you do that. Bring me despair,
you who want to tempt me into denying
the existence of our merciful Lord.
I came down here from pure mountain air in the Alps
to be among the people for a little longer
and share their problems but there was no open road,
just an aperture through thorny thickets . . .
I left a piece of clothing here and there
and got entangled in the shrubbery.
People gave in order to take back with interest . . .
They gave in order to turn gifts into debts . . .
People served you in order to command . . .
set you free in order to enslave you . . .
I lost my travelling companion along the way,
one trap followed upon the other
and I was sucked into mill-wheels,
came out the other end . . .
was shown a beacon in a child's eye . . .
which guided me to this place in the darkness.
And now you're handing me the bills.
What! He's gone as well.

I am alone!
In nocturnal darkness . . .

where the trees are fast asleep and the grass is weeping
with cold after the sun's gone down,
but the animals are keeping watch, not all, however.
The bat is plotting and the serpent wriggles
under poisonous mushrooms,
a badger, shunning the light, stirs
after a long day's sleep.
Alone! – Why? . . .
A traveller in other people's countries
is always a stranger, alone.
He passes through towns and villages,
puts up at hotels, checks out and moves on
until the journey is over . . . then he is home again!
But it's not over . . .
I can still hear . . . a dry branch
snapping . . . and an iron heel against the rock . . .
it's the formidable blacksmith
the idolater, with his flint knife . . .
he is looking for me . . .
and the miller with his mill-wheel
where I was sucked in
and almost got stuck . . .
The people of the shopping arcade
the people . . .
a net so easy to get caught in
but hard to escape from . . .
And the murderous Mr Möller . . .
with his bills and law suits
and alibis and libels
the man without honour . . .
What's that noise? It's music! I recognize the notes . . .
I recognize the notes . . . and your little hand
I have no desire to meet . . .
the fire is comfortably warm at a distance,
if you get too close, it will burn you.
And now: a child's voice in the dark!
You dear child, my last bright memory
that will follow me into the forest of the night,
on my final journey to the distant land,
The Land of Fulfilled Wishes,
which seemed like a mirage from the Alps
but vanished when I reached the valleys . . .
concealed by road dust . . . chimney smoke.

Where did you disappear to . . . lovely vision,
land of yearning and of dreams?

If only a vision, I want to see you once again,
from the snowy peak in the crystal clear air . . .
at the hermit's place . . . where I shall stay
and wait to be released . . .
I hope he'll make some space
under his cold white blanket:
and then he'll draw a fleeting epitaph in the snow:
'Here rests Ishmael, Hagar's son
once called Israel,
because he struggled with God
and didn't let go until overcome . . .
defeated by his omnipotent goodness'.

Oh eternal one! I won't let go of your hand,
your hard hand, unless you bless me!

Bless me, your poor mankind,
who suffers, suffers from your gift of life!
Me first who's suffered most
who's suffered most and grieved
because I couldn't be the man I'd hoped to be!

THE END